Watch me grow

Farm Animals

LONDON, NEW YORK, MUNICH,
MELBOURNE, and DELHI

Written and edited by Lisa Magloff
Designed by Leah Germann, Anthony Limerick,
Laura Roberts, Tory Gordon-Harris
DTP Designer Almudena Díaz
Picture Researcher Liz Moore
Production Emma Hughes

Jacket Design Hedi Gutt

Publishing Manager Sue Leonard
Managing Art Editor Clare Shedden

First American Edition, 2005

Published in the United States by
DK Publishing, Inc., 375 Hudson Street,
New York, New York 10014

06 07 08 09 10 9 8 7 6 5 4 3 2

A Cataloging-in-Publication record for this book
is available from the Library of Congress.

ISBN-13: 978-0-7566-1272-6
ISBN-10: 0-7566-1272-1

Color reproduction by Coloursystems
Printed and bound in China by South China Printing Co, Ltd

Discover more at
www.dk.com

Contents

I am a chick

I hatched out of an egg that
my mother laid. I pecked
my way out of the shell
with my beak. It was
very hard work.

The chick stays in
its egg for 21 days
before hatching.

Crack Crack Crack

Pecking for food

Chickens eat seeds, grain, and insects that they peck at with their hard beaks.

Cheep cheep cheep

Free at last!

Squeeze and push

Dry and fluffy

The hen keeps the chick warm until his feathers are dry and fluffy.

Growing into a rooster

My feathers are starting to change. When I am two weeks old, my adult feathers and my comb start to grow. Soon I will be a tall rooster.

Eight days old

Two weeks old

Four weeks old

Changing feathers
The chick's adult feathers are stronger and more waterproof.

cock-a-doodle-doo

Eight weeks old

Rooster
The rooster wakes
the farm up every
morning with his
loud crowing.

7

A little lamb

My twin brother and I are born in the spring. Mom keeps us warm and dry until our wool dries. After a few minutes, we are ready to stand up.

With Mom's help
The mother sheep cleans off the lambs. Then she helps them to their feet by gently nudging them with her nose.

we are warm

First drink

Lambs nurse standing up. The lambs will drink their mother's milk for about four months. The lambs will nurse twice a day until they are old enough to eat grass.

and cozy in this straw.

I'm two months old

I'm old enough to go outside and start eating tender grass. I stay close to Mom and bleat if I am in trouble. My woolly coat keeps me warm.

Sheep chew with the roof of their mouth.

Sheep have hooves that are split into two toes.

Woolly coat

The sheep grows a thick coat of wool every winter. In the spring, this wool is sheared off and made into yarn.

I live in a big field with my friends and family

In the field

Sheep spend most of their day outside in the field, looking for tender grass to eat.

Four little piglets have just been born

We are born in a cozy barn. Right away, we are ready to start eating and moving around, but we make sure to always stay close to Mom.

Newborn piglet

This piglet was the first one to be born. Mom has licked him clean. His eyes are already open, and in a few minutes he will be ready to stand up.

There's plenty of room for everyone

Time to get messy

We're four weeks old and we love to go outside. We root around in the grass, looking for food. A daily mud bath keeps bugs away.

The piglets will squeal if they need any help from Mom.

Pigs use their snouts to dig up roots to eat.

Home sweet home

Each pig family has its own small house, called an ark. At night, the family goes into its ark, where it's cozy and warm.

I love to snuffle around in the mud for tasty roots.

The little brown calf

When I am born, my mom cleans me with her rough tongue. I am hungry, but I need to stand up to feed. Mom gives me a helping nudge, and soon I can stand

Mom gives me a boost

Breakfast time

For the first six weeks, the calf will drink only his mother's milk. He stays close to his mom at all times.

I'm a bit wobbly...

The calf gets up one leg at a time.

I'm up at last!

Getting up

The calf leans forward with all his weight, and pushes his back legs straight. In no time at all, he's up on his feet.

In the green, grassy field

I'm three months old and now I can spend
my day with the other cows in our herd.
We all live together in a big field full
of grass and flowers.

This is me...
and my
best friend.

Cows are very
friendly and
like to live in
a big herd.

Chewing cud

Cows have a four-part stomach.
They can spit up their food
and chew it a second time.
This food is
called cud.

Cows can eat tough
grass and plants
because they
chew their food
over and over.

I love to chew grass all
day long—yum yum . . .

19

The circle of life
goes around
and around

... chick to chicken

Now you
know how
we grew from a ...

calf to cow ...

... lamb to sheep

... piglet to pig

Baah-bye!

21

Our farm friends from around the world

The Wyandotte chicken from the United States lays brown eggs.

Gloucester Old Spot pigs live in England and love to eat apples and acorns.

Ouch! Ouch!

Alsace pigs are from France and weigh more than a refrigerator!

Manx Longhorn sheep live on the Isle of Man and have very long horns.

Our farm friends from around the world come in lots of different sizes and shapes.

Wensleydale rams have very long, shaggy wool.

The Brahmin bull lives in hot places like India and Brazil.

I'm from Scotland.

cheep cheep

Aberdeen cows have long hair to protect them from the cold.

Farm facts

· ·

There are more chickens in the world than people.

China has more pigs than anywhere else in the world.

Sheep prefer to walk uphill, rather than downhill.

One cow makes enough manure each year to fill up your house.

Glossary

Beak
The hard, pointy part around the mouth that birds peck with.

Snout
The name for the long nose of some animals, including pigs.

Feather
A light, soft covering on a bird that keeps the bird warm.

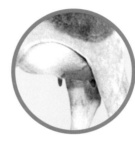

Udder
The part of the female cow that has the teats and gives milk.

Egg
Birds grow inside an egg until they hatch (are born).

Hoof
The hard part of the foot of some animals, such as pigs and horses.

Acknowledgments
The publisher would like to thank the following for their kind permission to reproduce their photographs:
Key: t = top, b = bottom, l = left, r = right, bkgrd = background, c = center

Alamy/Juniors Bildarchiv: 2-3, /David Noton Photography: 11b, Archivberlin Fotoagentur GmbH/Bildagentur Geduldig: 14, 21 pig tl, /Minden Mas: 22-23b; Corbis/Najlah Feanny-Hicks: 10tr, /Ted Spiegel: 12-13, /Papilio/Steve Austin: 15t, /Robert Dowling 22tl, /David Katzenstein: 23tr;

Country Life Picture Library/Joe Cornish: 16tl; Ecoscene/Angela Hampton: 8r, 9t, b, 21 lamb bl; Eye Ubiquitous/Hutchison: 8l; Getty Images/Image Bank/Cesar Lucas: 1, /Taxi/VCL: 4-5, /David Noton: 18l, 20 cow tr, /Stone/Tony Page: 7 bkgrd, /Peter Cade: 15b, 18-19c, /Photographer's Choice/Mike Hill: 7tr, /Lester Lefkowitz: 19r; Jeff Moore courtesy Wood & Sons of Hawkhurst: 10br.

All other pictures © Dorling Kindersley Media Library